KENTUCKY BASKETBALL

DARCY PATTISON

rosen publishing's
rosen
central®

New York

Published in 2014 by The Rosen Publishing Group, Inc.
29 East 21st Street, New York, NY 10010

First Edition

Library of Congress Cataloging-in-Publication Data

Pattison, Darcy.
Kentucky basketball/by Darcy Pattison.
     p. cm.—(America's most winning teams)
Includes bibliographical references and index.
ISBN 978-1-4488-9403-1 (library binding)—ISBN 978-1-4488-9431-4 (pbk.)—
ISBN 978-1-4488-9432-1 (6-pack)
1.University of Kentucky—Basketball—History_Juvenile literature. 2. Kentucky Wildcats (Basketball team—History —Juvenile literature. 3. Kentucky Wildcats (Basketball team)—History. I. Title.
GV885.43.U53 P38 2014
796.32363—d23

Manufactured in the United States of America

CPSIA Compliance Information: Batch #S13YA: For further information, contact Rosen Publishing, New York, New York, at 1-800-237-9932.

CONTENTS

INTRODUCTION

It was Valentine's Day 1938. Packed into the University of Kentucky Alumni Gym were over four thousand people, some sitting in windows, others hanging from the rafters. The University of Kentucky Wildcat basketball team led the top-ranked Marquette University team by ten points. In the second half, though, Marquette's methodical play slowly gained points until they led. Once, twice, the Wildcats fought back to a slim lead, only to lose it again. With fifteen seconds left in the game, the score was 33–33. And the ball came to Joe "Red" Hagan.

The *Lexington Herald* reported, "He felt it, and so did all those fans who saw Red, a devout Catholic, kneel in the middle of the floor, bless himself, mumble a prayer, and then bless himself again."

Hagan's shot from near midcourt banked off the backboard and went through the net. Though Marquette had four more shots, they missed them all. Game over. Kentucky—35, Marquette—33.

Now comes the most amazing part of this story. Among the frantic fans was Kentucky Governor A. B. "Happy" Chandler. He was so elated with the Kentucky win that he called for a hammer and nail. He found the exact spot for Red Hagan's hoop and hammered the nail into the floor.

Kentucky basketball began in February 1903, when the university was known as the State College. Since then, it has become the winningest basketball team in NCAA (National Collegiate Athletic Association) history: eight NCAA championships

Captain and star center Alex "the Beak" Groza scored 17 points as the Fabulous Five defeated Columbia 76–53 in the Eastern Regional NCAA tournament. He played in all thirty-nine games of the 1947–48 season.

(1947–48, 1948–49, 1950–51, 1957–58, 1977–78, 1995–96, 1997–98, 2011–12), forty-six all-American players, and over two thousand wins. This is the amazing story of the University of Kentucky Wildcats basketball team.

CHAPTER 1

THE BIG BLUE PLAYS TO WIN

The University of Kentucky, more than any other college basketball program, wants to be the best of the best. Why? How did this ambition get instilled into the program, into the fans—seemingly into the very courts and balls of the program?

There was always a hunger to win, but when Adolph Rupp took over the team in 1930, he embodied the desire to win. His fire to win took time to take hold: he refined his game plan of strict man-to-man defense and a fast-paced running game. Finally, in 1948, he coached the Fabulous Five, a team that could run his game to perfection: junior guard Ralph Beard, senior Kenny Rollins, junior center Alex "the Beak" Groza, and junior forwards Wallace "Wah Wah" Jones and Cliff Barker. They swept the NCAA championships that year, playing with ruthless precision. The same team took gold at the 1948 Summer Olympics in London.

Something about winning, about Rupp's about years of building to this moment, of growing the fan base to expect wins, made the attitude stick. Rupp's teams took the national championships in 1949 and 1951. They were at the top, and they liked it at the top.

But then disaster struck. During a 1949 National Invitational Tournament (NIT), three players—Ralph Beard, Alex Groza, and Dale Barnstable—had accepted bribes

Coach Rupp, #45 Cliff Berger, #42 Pat Riley, and #55 Thad Jaracz. The 1965–66 team had no player taller than 6'5" (1.96 m), and they were known as Rupp's Runts.

of $500 each to shave points in a game against Loyola. This means that they still played to win the game, but they deliberately missed baskets or didn't take shots so that they won by only a certain number of points. Gamblers bet on the basketball games, not just on which team would win, but by how much. Eventually thirty-two players from seven colleges who fixed eighty-six games between 1947 and 1950 were arrested. But with Kentucky's three players accepting bribes, the NCAA gave its first ever "death penalty." In other words, it forced Kentucky to cancel its 1952–53 season. It was ineligible for any after-season games.

Sports Illustrated reported that Coach Rupp had bragged that his team was untouchable: "They couldn't reach my boys with a ten-foot pole." For over twenty years, his anger at the guilty players burned and he refused to speak to them.

But Rupp also had a basketball team to rebuild, and in 1958, Kentucky came back to win its fourth NCAA championship. The Fiddlin' Five went into the tournament with no height, no playmaker, and little speed. But the players did the best they could. Forward Johnny Cox had a great perimeter shot. Guard Adrian Smith wasn't flashy, but he was a consistent scorer. Center Ed Beck could pull down rebounds. Bowlegged guard Vernon Hatton shot well from the inside. And John Crigler could draw a foul, then make his free throws.

Rupp finished his forty-two-year reign as UK's head basketball coach with four national championships.

FOUR MORE NCAA WINS

In 1973, Rupp retired and was replaced by his longtime assistant, Joe B. Hall (1973–1985). Hall had, perhaps, the hardest job ever—to replace a legend. He began by instituting the Midnight Special to drum up fan support. It was a free, open practice that started at 12:01 AM on the first day that the NCAA allowed teams to practice. An instant tradition, it bolstered Hall's coaching and he led the team to an NCAA championship in 1978.

Under head coach Eddie Sutton (1986–1989), scandal again rocked the University of Kentucky team. Boosters and alumni were accused of providing cash to recruits and players. Eric Manual, a Wildcat recruit, was accused of cheating on the ACT college entrance examination. The NCAA stripped UK of several scholarships and banned it from television and postseason play. Coach Sutton and his assistant coaches resigned, and key players transferred.

The University of Kentucky brought in Coach Rick Pitino (1990–1997) to rebuild the program. It was a return to the glory days, with a 1995 NCAA Championship, the UK's sixth. The seventh championship came in 1998 for Coach Tubby Smith's (1998–2007) Comeback Cats.

A 2006 NCAA ruling changed the face of college basketball. The "one-and-done" rule said that high school players had to play at least one year of college ball before they could be eligible for the National Basketball Association (NBA) draft. That meant the top young

Coach Pitino and Rodrick Rhodes (#12). Rhodes, known as the high school "Beast of the East" from Jersey City, New Jersey, called Pitino, "the god of coaches."

players wanted to play one and only one year before turning professional. Why risk injuries in a longer college career? Why not go for the high-dollar career right away?

Coach John Calipari (2009–present) took advantage of the rule to recruit the best high school players with the promise of lots of playing time as freshmen. That would give them the opportunity to develop as players and attract NBA recruiters. It paid off with a 2012 Final Four team, led by freshmen Anthony Davis and Michael Kidd-Gilchrist. Kentucky fans would not be content with just a second Final Four appearance in two years.

As a college coach, John Calipari has eighteen twenty-win seasons, eight thirty-win seasons, and has been named National Coach of the Year three times.

Even the players knew what was expected of them: a win.

"Coach Cal tells us: Kentucky's not for everyone," freshman Anthony Davis said in an interview with the *Courier-Journal* newspaper. "He says the people who come here are built for this."

Maybe that's the difference with Kentucky teams, each player is built to win. The whole system at UK is built to create a place where basketball players can thrive and fans can watch action-packed, thrilling moments of their beloved Big Blue team. It worked out in 2012, when Kentucky won its eighth NCAA championship over the Louisville Cardinals 69–61.

Kentucky is the winningest college basketball team with 2,090 wins, as of the end of the 2012 season. It has survived NCAA death penalties, NCAA probations, and lean years with poor talent or poor coaching. But through it all, the passion to win has remained strong in the fans, coaches, and players. The University of Kentucky doesn't just play basketball; it plays to win. It always has, and it always will.

CHAPTER 2

NCAA CHAMPIONSHIP COACHES

James Naismith, who invented basketball in 1891, didn't think coaches were important. Instead, Forrest "Phog" Allen is credited as the father of basketball coaching. According to *Sports Illustrated* reporter Frank DeFord, Naismith once told Allen, "You don't coach this game, Forrest, you just play it." Allen replied, "Well, you can teach them to pass at angles and run in curves." As the sport of basketball developed, coaches have done far more than just teach passing and running. These five men took the Kentucky Wildcats to eight NCAA Championships.

THE BARON OF BLUEGRASS: ADOLPH RUPP, HEAD BASKETBALL COACH 1931–72

RECORD: 42 SEASONS, 876 WINS, 82.2 PERCENT WIN RECORD.

6 NCAA FINAL FOUR, 4 NCAA CHAMPIONSHIPS IN 1948, 49, 51, 58.

INDUCTED INTO NAISMITH MEMORIAL BASKETBALL HALL OF FAME IN 1968.

Adolph Rupp (1901–1977), a German American, was born in Halstead, Kansas, on September 2, 1901, just

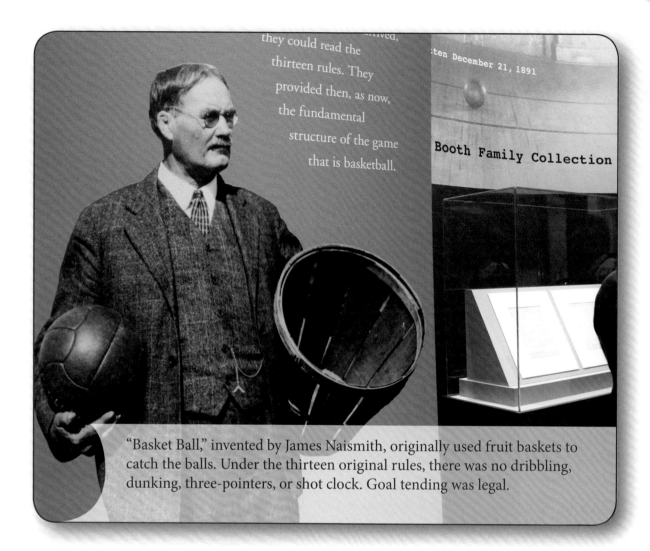

they could read the thirteen rules. They provided then, as now, the fundamental structure of the game that is basketball.

:ten December 21, 1891

Booth Family Collection

"Basket Ball," invented by James Naismith, originally used fruit baskets to catch the balls. Under the thirteen original rules, there was no dribbling, dunking, three-pointers, or shot clock. Goal tending was legal.

ten years after Naismith invented basketball. When Adolph was four years old, his brothers nailed a basket to a barn wall. His mother stuffed rags into gunnysacks, creating a rough, round ball that didn't bounce or dribble. But the Rupp boys practiced shooting. Adolph Rupp's high school team won state championships in 1908 and 1909. Then Rupp went to the University of Kansas, where Phog Allen was coaching and Jim Naismith was the assistant coach.

Rupp graduated in 1923, coached a few years of high school football, and in 1930, applied for a coaching job at the University of Kentucky. From 1903–1930, the University of Kentucky had employed fifteen coaches and was looking for someone to stay a while. Hired in 1930, Rupp stayed for the next forty-two seasons.

Superstitious, he always wore double-breasted brown suits to a game and chewed a stick of Beechmont gum. At the time, basketball coaches stressed a slow, deliberate style of ball handling. Rupp's style, though, emphasized speed, screens, precise passing, and good rebounding.

Ultimately, his teams won NCAA basketball championships in 1948, 1949, 1951, and 1958. Five of his players anchored the 1948 Olympic basketball team that won gold medals. During his time at Kentucky, his teams won 876 times, making him the winningest coach ever; today, he is still the fifth winningest coach.

At seventy years old, Rupp retired in 1972. He died on December 10, 1977, and was buried in one of his famous brown suits.

CHAMPION PLAYER, CHAMPION COACH: JOE B. HALL 1973–85

RECORD: OVER 13 SEASONS, 297 WINS, 74.8 PERCENT WIN RECORD. 3 NCAA FINAL FOUR, NCAA CHAMPIONSHIP IN 1978.

Joe Beasman Hall was born on November 30, 1928, in Cynthiana, Kentucky, just twenty minutes north of the University of Kentucky campus. He played on the 1949 "Fabulous Five" Kentucky NCAA championship team, then finished his basketball career at the University of the South (Sewanee). He toured with

Joe B. Hall coached the Wildcats for thirteen years for a 297-100 record and the 1978 NCAA championship. He was named National Coach of the Year in 1978.

the Harlem Globetrotters for the 1951 season before returning to the University of Kentucky, where he graduated in 1955.

He coached high school ball and college ball in Colorado and Missouri, then returned to Kentucky as an assistant coach in 1965. After seven years, he replaced Adolph Rupp in1973. Everyone agreed that his was the hardest coaching job because he was replacing a legend.

Hall's team won the 1978 NCAA Championship. Hall became one of only three men to win an NCAA Championship both as a player and as a coach. The others were Bobby Knight and Dean Smith.

REBUILDING A DYNASTY: RICK PITINO 1990-97

RECORD: 8 SEASONS, 219 WINS, 81.4 PERCENT WIN RECORD. 3 NCAA FINAL FOUR, NCAA CHAMPIONSHIP IN 1995.

Rick Pitino, a Sicilian American, was born on September 18, 1952, in New York, New York. He captained his St. Dominic high school team in Oyster Bay, Long Island. He played college ball for the University of Massachusetts Amherst team as a guard. His 329 career assists rank tenth all-time at UMass, as of the 2009–2010 season.

When Pitino stepped into the University of Kentucky head coach position, the team was on NCAA probation from recruiting problems under Coach Eddie Sutton. Pitino rebuilt the team using a full-court, pressure defense. In 1993, they went to the NCAA Final Four and only lost to Michigan in overtime. They returned in 1995 to win the NCAA Championship. Pitino left Kentucky to coach the NBA's Boston Celtics, then returned to college ball in 2001 as the head coach at the University of Louisville.

LIST OF ALL UNIVERSITY OF KENTUCKY BASKETBALL HEAD COACHES

YEARS	NAME(S)	TENURE	WON - LOST	PCT.	BEST SEASON
1903–09	W. W. H. Mustaine and Others	7	21-35	.375	
1910	E. R. Sweetland and R. E. Spahr	1	4-8	.333	
1911	H. J. Iddings	1	5-6	.454	5-6 in 1911
1912	E. R. Sweetland	1	9-0	1.000	9-0 in 1912
1913	J. J. Tigert	1	5-3	.625	5-3 in 1913
1914–15	Alpha Brumage	2	19-7	.731	12-2 in 1914
1916	J. J. Tigert (James Fark)	1	8-6	.571	8-6 in 1916
1917	J. J. Tigert (W. P. Tuttle)	1	4-6	.400	4-6 in 1917
1918	S. A. Bole	1	9-2-1	.792	9-2-1 in 1918
1919	Andrew Gill	1	6-8	.428	6-8 in 1919
1920–24	George Buchheit	5	44-27	.619	13-1 in 1921
1925	C. O. Applegran	1	13-8	.619	13-8 in 1925
1926	Ray Eklund	1	15-3	.833	15-3 in 1926
1927	Basil Hayden	1	13-3	.187	3-13 in 1927
1929–30	John Mauer	3	40-14	.740	16-3 in 1930
1931–72	Adolph Rupp	+42	876-190	.822	25-0 in 1954
1973–85	Joe B. Hall	13	297-100	.748	30-2 in 1978
1986–89	Eddie Sutton	4	88-39	.693	32-4 in 1986
1990–97	Rick Pitino	8	219-50	.814	34-2 in 1996
1998–07	Orlando "Tubby" Smith	9	241-71	.772	35-4 in 1998
2008–09	Billy Gillespie	2	40-27	.597	24-14 in 2009
2009–current	John Calipari	4	102-14	.879	38-2, in 2012

TUBBYBALL: TUBBY SMITH, 1998–2007

RECORD: 16 SEASONS, 387 WINS, 72.7 PERCENT WIN RECORD. 1 NCAA FINAL FOUR, NCAA CHAMPIONSHIP IN 1998

Sixth of seventeen children, Orlando "Tubby" Smith was born on June 30, 1951, to sharecroppers Guffrie and Parthenia

Coach Tubby Smith speaks with player Derrick Jasper (#5). Besides his coaching career at four universities, Smith served as the assistant coach for the gold-medal 2000 U.S. Olympic men's basketball team in Sydney, Australia.

Smith. His family nicknamed him Tubby because he loved to take baths in the family's galvanized washtub. He played basketball for High Point College, North Carolina, and married the homecoming queen, Donna. He served as an assistant coach under Rick Pitino before moving as head coach to the University of Tulsa and University of Georgia. In 1997, he returned to Kentucky as head basketball coach.

Smith's team played a slower defense-oriented game that was dubbed Tubbyball. His 1998 team, the Comeback Cats, won the NCAA championship. It was the only team in over twenty years to win without a first team all-American or future NBA recruit. In 2007, Tubby Smith became head coach at the University of Minnesota.

ONE-AND-DONE TEAMS: JOHN CALIPARI 2009–PRESENT

RECORD (AS OF 2012 SEASON): 102 WINS, 87.9 PERCENT WIN RECORD.

2 NCAA FINAL FOUR, NCAA CHAMPIONSHIP IN 2012.

John Calipari, an Italian American, was born on February 10, 1959, in a suburb of Pittsburgh, Pennsylvania. His father worked at the airport, refueling planes. Calipari played college ball for North Carolina–Wilmington and Clarion State. He began his coaching career as an assistant volunteer under Kansas coach Ted Owens. He coached at Philadelphia, UMass, and Memphis State before moving to the University of Kentucky in 2009.

Calipari's success at Kentucky has been partly because he takes advantage of the 2006 NCAA rule called "one-and-done." It forces high school players to play at least one year of college ball before they are eligible for the NBA draft.

Calipari recruits the best high school players, promising them lots of playing time as freshmen, which allows them to have an immediate impact, which turns into a better NBA draft spot. In 2010, he lost five players to the NBA first-round draft, including the number one choice, John Wall. That 2010 team was nicknamed the Draft Cats. Following the 2012 NCAA Championship, members of the Eighth Wonder team were also drafted by the NBA. Anthony Davis was the number one draft pick, and Michael Kidd-Gilchrist was the number two draft pick.

CHAPTER 3

FAMOUS GAMES

I n the history of any sport, there are some games that stand out for various reasons. Some games are important just because they represent the first of some kind.

HISTORIC FIRSTS

The first University of Kentucky basketball team was created a mere twelve years after James Naismith invented the game. In other words, in just a dozen years, the sport had spread so widely that a college could organize a team and expect to have other opponents to play. On February 13, 1903, State University of Kentucky (renamed University of Kentucky in 1916) played the Lexington YMCA, winning 11-10. The Wildcats finished the first season with a 1-2 record.

By March 1921, basketball had become widespread enough to be included in the Southern Intercollegiate Athletic Association (SIAA). The SIAA organized the first college basketball tournament ever played, with teams from Tulane, Mercer, Mississippi A&M, Georgia, and Kentucky. Basketball was already a winning tradition in Kentucky and hundreds of fans gathered in the historic Phoenix hotel in downtown Lexington, Kentucky. As the play-by-play of the game was received

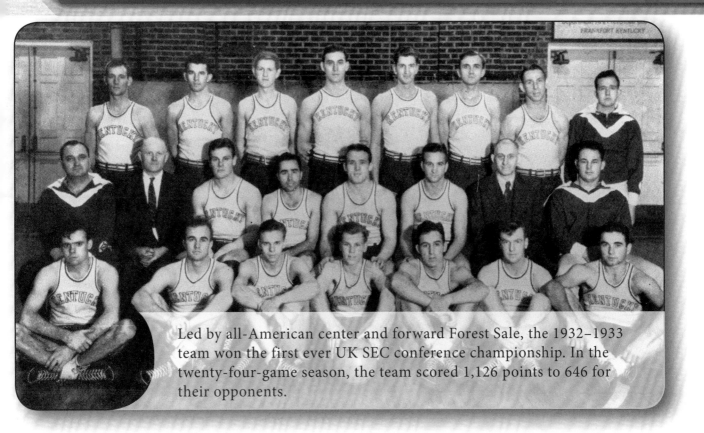

Led by all-American center and forward Forest Sale, the 1932–1933 team won the first ever UK SEC conference championship. In the twenty-four-game season, the team scored 1,126 points to 646 for their opponents.

by telegraph, an announcer would read the message to the crowd. When Kentucky defeated Georgia, 20–19, on a foul shot taken after the final whistle, the team was heralded by all as "one of the greatest basketball machines in the history of the South."

A HEARTBREAKING LOSS

While each season brings games that people predict will live in the memory of sports fans, there are some games that truly stand out above the rest. On March 28, 1992, Rick Pitino's team lost what many call the best NCAA tournament game ever played.

The 1992 NCAA tournament East Regional Finals in Philadelphia put Kentucky up against Mike Krzyzewski's

Duke's Christian Laettner shoots the game-winning basket in overtime over Kentucky's Deron Deldhuas to win the "greatest college basketball game ever played," with the "most memorable basketball shot of all-time."

Duke University Blue Devils, the defending NCAA champions. For two and a half hours, the teams battled back and forth, each team shooting over 61 percent from the field. Christian Laettner of Duke shot ten of ten field goals and ten of ten fouls, giving him an amazingly perfect night. The game went to a heart-stopping overtime and with only 2.1 seconds left, Kentucky led. Coach Pitino, however, told his players to back off and not foul, leaving Christian Laettner unguarded. When the ball was inbounded, Grant Hill shoveled a 75-foot (23-meter) pass to Christian Laettner, who shot a 17-footer (5-meter) at the buzzer. Game over: Duke 104, Kentucky 103. Kentucky fans were heartbroken; Duke fans were elated that their team was heading to the Final Four.

INTEGRATING BASKETBALL

A different kind of "first" basketball game happened on March 19, 1966, in an NCAA championship game against Texas Western (now University of Texas–El Paso, or UTEP). Kentucky started five white players, while Texas Western started five black players. This was a time when the civil rights movement was starting around the country and the contrast between the teams was striking. It was the beginning of awareness of the need to integrate college sports teams. In 1969, the University of Kentucky signed its first black player, Tom Payne, an athletic center out of Louisville, Kentucky.

FANTASTIC WIN: THE GREATEST COMEBACK

On February 15, 1994, the NCAA tournament was in full swing, but the Kentucky Wildcats were in a slump, losing four games in a row. Rick Pitino's team couldn't hit anything against Louisiana State University (LSU). At almost the five-minute mark, UK finally scored its first field goal. Pitino benched three players, with a mass substitution, but that didn't help much. LSU led 48–42 at the half, with Kentucky shooting only 39 percent, a miserable first-half field goal percentage.

It got worse. With less than sixteen minutes left, the Wildcats were down 68–37. Desperate, Kentucky started focusing on three-point shots and closed the lead some. With such a large lead, LSU started making sloppy mistakes, which helped the Wildcats even more. With only two minutes left, the Wildcats had pulled to 93–90. Then LSU hit a huge basket: 95–90. Kentucky answered with a three-pointer: 95–93. But LSU turned the ball over, giving the Wildcats a chance. With only nineteen seconds left, it was Kentucky 96, LSU 95. It was back and forth, until at 2.2 seconds left in the game, Kentucky hit two free throws to go ahead 99–95. The game stands as the greatest collegiate comeback game ever and is often referred to as the "Mardi Gras Miracle" because the game was played in New Orleans, home of the famous Mardi Gras celebrations.

THE FUTURE OF BASKETBALL?

When the University of Kentucky and University of Kansas met in the NCAA 2012 Championship game, it was a blue

Michael Kidd-Gilchrist (#14) and Kansas Jeff Withhey (#5). In the 2012 NBA draft, Kidd-Gilchrist was taken as the number two pick at the age of nineteen.

versus blue contest between winners. In the history of the sport, Kentucky had won more games than any other team, at 2,089 wins. But Kansas was nipping at their heels as the second-ranked team overall, with 2,070 wins. They were almost matched in Final Four appearances, with Kentucky fifteen, Kansas fourteen.

This game, though, was complicated by the NBA's 2006 ruling on high school players' eligibility to play professional ball. The so-called "one-and-done" ruling forces players to play at least one year of college ball before turning pro. Coach John Calipari of Kentucky had packed talented freshmen on his team, knowing that they would be there only one year. These young players had a lot on the line, especially how much money they would make next year in the NBA. In the end, Kentucky easily defeated Louisville 67–59. But some wonder if this game didn't change the future of college basketball by emphasizing the young rising stars over the seniors who had fought for a spot on the team for four years.

On December 21, 2009, Kentucky became the first program in college basketball history to reach the two-thousand-win plateau. As of the end of 2012 season, they had won 2,090 games.

CHAPTER 4

BASKETBALL HALL OF FAMERS

Over the 110 years of University of Kentucky basketball, there have been more than one thousand players. Of these, five have been inducted into the Naismith Memorial Basketball Hall of Fame. Here are their stories.

CLIFF HAGAN: A WICKED HOOK SHOT

BORN: DECEMBER 9, 1931, IN OWENSBORO, KENTUCKY

6'4" (193 CM), 210 LBS (95 KG), SMALL FORWARD/GUARD, JERSEY #6, 17, 16

ALL-AMERICAN 1952, 1954

NCAA CHAMPIONSHIP AT UNIVERSITY OF KENTUCKY, 1954

DRAFTED NUMBER THIRTEEN OVERALL IN THIRD ROUND OF 1953 NBA DRAFT BY BOSTON CELTICS

NBA ALL STAR 1958–1962

INAUGURAL ABA ALL-STAR

NBA CAREER: 840 PROFESSIONAL GAMES, 14,870 POINTS (17.7 PPG), REBOUNDS 5,555 (6.6RPG), ASSISTS 2.646 (3.2 APG)

Cliff Hagan starred at the University of Kentucky and for thirteen professional seasons with the NBA's St.

Cliff Hagan's nickname during his ten-year NBA career was "L'il Abner," a reference to a comic strip about hillbillies. It was a joke about coming from the hill country of Kentucky.

Louis Hawks and the ABA's Dallas Chaparrals. In 1954, he led the Kentucky Wildcats to an 86-5 record, including a 25-0 season in 1954.

Hagan was known for his hook shot, his speed, and strength. In a March 31, 2011, interview on the *Sports and Torts* radio show, Hagan said, "The hook shot is a lost art." He explained that it is an alien shot to anything else you do with a basketball because it's not just pushing a ball. It's like a layup with a finger roll. Hagan suspects the hook shot is rare because it takes so much patience to learn. Hagan worked for six to eight years during high school and college to develop and perfect his hook shot. He was inducted into the Hall of Fame in 1978.

FORTY-TWO RETIRED JERSEYS

In recognition of outstanding contributions to the University of Kentucky basketball program, the University of Kentucky Athletics Department has a tradition of retiring jerseys. That means the number on the jersey cannot ever be worn again by a UK player. There is a five-year waiting period after leaving the university to be eligible for inclusion into the University of Kentucky Hall of Fame, and a ten-year waiting period to have a jersey retired. An individual must be a member of the Hall of Fame to be eligible for jersey retirement. These players (and coaches) were honored with retired jerseys.

Basil Hayden
56 - Burgess Carey
Carey Spicer
Adolph Rupp, Head Coach
Forest "Aggie" Sale
7 - John "Frenchy" DeMoisey
4 - Layton "Michey" Rouse
26 - Kenny Rallins+
15 - Alex Groza+
12 - Ralph Beard+
27 - Wallace Jones+
22 - Cliff Barker+
77 - Bill Spivey
30 - Frank Ramsey*
6 - Cliff Hagan*
16 - Lou Tsioropoulos*

42 - Bill Evans*
20 - Gayle Rose*
Caywood Ledford - "Voice of the Wildcats"
22 - Jerry Bird*
44 - Phil Grawemeyer*
50 - Bob Burrow
52 - Vernon Hatton
24 - Johnny Cox
Bill Keightley "Mr. Wildcat" - Equipment Manager
44 - Cotton Nash
10 - Louie Dampier
42 - Pat Riley
44 - Dan Issel

*Member of 1954 Undefeated National Champions
+Member of "The Fabulous Five," 1948 National Champions & Olympic Gold Medalists

Joe B. Hall, Head Coach
35 - Kevin Grevey
21 - Jack Givens
53 - Rick Robey
4 - Kyle Macy
34 - Kenny Walker

32 - Richie Farmer
12 - Deron Feldhaus
34 - John Pelphrey
11 - Sean Woods
24 - Jamal Mashburn
Rick Pitino, Head Coach

*Member of 1954 Undefeated National Champions
+Member of "The Fabulous Five," 1948 National Champions & Olympic Gold Medalists

FRANK RAMSEY: THE SIXTH MAN

BORN: JULY 13, 1931, IN CORYDON, KENTUCKY

6' 3", 190 LBS (86 KG), SMALL FORWARD/GUARD, JERSEY #23

NCAA CHAMPIONSHIP AT UNIVERSITY OF KENTUCKY, 1951

ALL-AMERICAN 1952, 1954

DRAFTED NUMBER FIVE OVERALL IN FIRST ROUND OF THE 1953 NBA DRAFT BY BOSTON CELTICS

NBA CHAMPIONSHIP WITH BOSTON CELTICS, 1957, 1959–64

NBA CAREER: POINTS 8,378 (13.4PPG), REBOUNDS 3,410 (5.5RPG), ASSISTS 1134 (1,8APG)

COACHED THE ABA'S KENTUCKY COLONELS, 1970–71

Frank Ramsey was known during his years at the University of Kentucky as the Kentucky Colonel. He led the Kentucky Wildcats to a 32-2 record in 1951 and a perfect 25-0 season in 1954. He played nine professional seasons for the Boston Celtics, where he was given a unique role. Most teams have five starters and then a bench of subs. Ramsey didn't want to be a starter, but he also wanted to contribute to the overall game. He became the first "sixth man," a strong player who is saved until late in the game, when he can come in fresh and turn the game around. Ramsey was a confident, thoughtful player who excelled in high-pressure situations and had a knack for coming through in a clutch. He was inducted in 1981.

DANIEL P. "DAN" ISSEL: HARD WORK

BORN: OCTOBER 24, 1948, IN BATAVIA, ILLINOIS

6'8" (203 CM), 240 LBS (108 KG), CENTER/POWER FORWARD, JERSEY #44, TWENTY-FIVE

ALL-AMERICAN, 1970

DRAFTED NUMBER 122 OVERALL IN EIGHTH ROUND OF THE 1970 NBA DRAFT BY DETROIT PISTONS

ABA CO-ROOKIE OF THE YEAR, 1971

ABA CHAMPIONSHIP WITH KENTUCKY COLONELS, 1975

NBA ALL-STAR, 1977

ABA AND NBA CAREER: POINTS 27,842 (22.6PPG), REBOUNDS 11,133 (9.1RPG), ASSISTS 2,907 (2.4 APG)

Dan Issel was never a star, not in his years at the University of Kentucky, not in his fifteen professional seasons in the NBA/ABA. Instead, he was known as the Horse, a hard-working player who never gave up. He had a smooth, accurate outside shot and outran opponents regularly. He could head fake with the best and had a good drive to the hoop. He had a reliable jump shot from 15 feet (5 yards). The list of his abilities goes on, but everyone agreed that in a one-on-one contest, he would never

Freshmen Dan Issel (*right*) and Mike Casey fly high as Coach Rupp watches. His freshman season, Issel scored 444 points; by his senior year, he more than doubled that with 948 points.

come out on top. Instead, his best quality was his willingness to work and to work hard. The NBA said, "Issel earned his place in NBA history by hustling and squeezing the most out of his talents."

Issel managed to squeeze out an amazing set of records. At the University of Kentucky, he set twenty-three school records, including most points and rebounds. In his last season with the Denver Nuggets, Issel was the Nuggets' leader in points and second in rebounding. He was inducted in 1993.

PAT RILEY: TEAM WORK

BORN: MARCH 20, 1945, IN ROME, NEW YORK

6'4" (193 CM), 205 LBS (93 KG), GUARD, FORWARD, JERSEY # 42, 12

DRAFTED NUMBER SEVEN OVERALL IN THE FIRST ROUND OF THE 1967 NBA DRAFT BY SAN DIEGO CLIPPERS

NBA CAREER: POINTS 3,906 (7.4PPG), REBOUNDS 855 (1.6RPG), ASSISTS 913 (1.7 APG)

THREE-TIME NBA COACH OF THE YEAR 1990, 1993, 1997

NAMED ONE OF THE GREATEST HEAD COACHES IN NBA HISTORY, 1996

NBA COACH OF THE MONTH FOR A RECORD ELEVEN TIMES

UK forward Pat Riley (#42) shoots over a Tennessee player. Riley later said that what he learned at Kentucky was how to be a competitor.

At the University of Kentucky, Pat Riley was named an all-American and the 1965–66 SEC Player of the Year. During his nine professional seasons, the L.A. Lakers took the national championship in 1972. But Riley was inducted into the Naismith Memorial Basketball Hall of Fame more for his work as an NBA coach, where he led teams to six more national championships (1980, 1982, 1985, 1987, 1988, and 2006).

Riley's coaching style has been called "showtime" because he emphasized fast breaks and no-look passing. But his real strength was emphasizing the power of teamwork. "I'm a tremendous believer in peer pressure," Riley said in a 1987 *Washington Post* interview. "I look at our team as a big circle with twelve parts and I'm on the perimeter just trying to make sure it stays enclosed. It's OK for a player to have space and to get out on a limb at times, but he has to be aware of the others and that they will pull him back in."

Riley is still one of the winningest coaches in NBA history. He was inducted into the Hall of Fame in 2008.

ADRIAN "ODIE" SMITH: "BLESSED BEYOND MY WILDEST DREAMS."

BORN: OCTOBER 6, 1936, IN FARMINGTON, KENTUCKY

6'1" (185 CM), 180 LBS (181 KG), POINT GUARD, JERSEY #10

1958 NCAA CHAMPIONSHIP TEAM

U.S. ARMED FORCES BASKETBALL TEAM WHILE SERVING IN THE MILITARY

U.S. OLYMPIC TEAM, WENT UNDEFEATED THROUGH THE 1960 ROME, ITALY, OLYMPICS, 8–0

DRAFTED NUMBER EIGHTY-SIX OVERALL IN THE FIFTEENTH ROUND OF THE 1958 NBA DRAFT BY CINCINNATI ROYALS

NBA AND ABA CAREER: POINTS 8,750 (11.3 PPG), REBOUNDS 1,626 (2.1 RPG), ASSISTS 1,739 (2.3 APG)

Adrian Smith almost didn't play basketball because he had no way to get home after high school practices. That is, until his high school principal offered to drive him home each day. He played two seasons at the University of Kentucky, including the 1958 NCAA Championship team. Though he was drafted by the Cincinnati Royals, Smith joined the army instead. Playing on the U.S. Armed Forces basketball team helped him make the 1960 Olympic team, at a time when only amateurs were eligible.

About the Olympic gold medal, Smith told KentuckySports.com, "As much as playing at Kentucky and winning a national championship at Kentucky meant to me, that was the highlight of my basketball career. That was winning for your country."

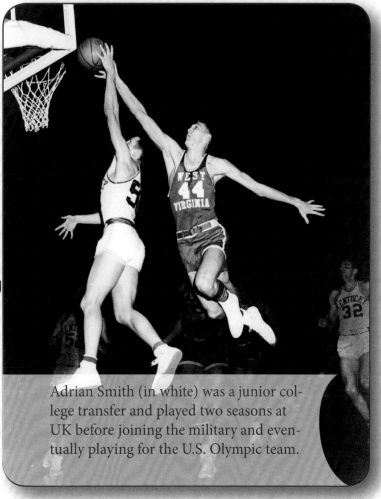

Adrian Smith (in white) was a junior college transfer and played two seasons at UK before joining the military and eventually playing for the U.S. Olympic team.

In his eleven seasons of professional basketball, 1966 stands out in Smith's memory because he was named the NBA All-Star Game Most Valuable Player (MVP). To this day, he is the only former Kentucky Wildcat to win that award. Smith still has the blue Ford Galaxy that was awarded to the 1966 All-Star MVP. Speaking to KentuckySports.com about his career in basketball, Smith said, "It's hard to put into words. I've been blessed beyond my wildest dreams." He was inducted in 2012, as part of the 1960 Olympic team.

CHAPTER 5

WILDCAT TRADITIONS

In 1982, Coach Joe B. Hall searched for a way to boost the fan support for the Kentucky Wildcats team. He remembered that in 1971, Maryland coach Lefty Dreisell held a special practice at midnight on the first day when college teams could begin preseason practices. In October 1982, the first Midnight Special at Kentucky drew more than 8,500 fans to the free open practice. Of course, it started at 12:01 AM.

Since that first midnight practice, Kentucky has developed a rich tradition of Big Blue Madness events, each year getting bigger and more spectacular. In 1994, leather-clad Coach Rick Pitino entered Rupp Arena on a Harley-Davidson motorcycle to the tune of "Born to Be Wild." The next year, Walter McCarty and Tony Delk became "Catman" and "Robin," swooping down on rope to land on the court. The women's basketball team was included in the celebration, starting in 2003 with the introduction of the new women's head basketball coach, Mickie DeMoss. In 2009, John Wall danced in the rafters. In 2011, women's basketball Coach Matthew Mitchell dressed and danced like Michael Jackson to the song "Billy Jean."

When the NCAA changed its rules in 2005, they changed the flavor of the Midnight Madness. Now teams are allowed to hold their first practice at 7 PM on the closest Friday to October 15, the official start of the men's

Freshman Archie Goodwin, a 6'5" (1.95 m) guard who was recruited from Sylvan Hills, Arkansas, dunks a ball during the Big Blue Madness practice and celebration on Friday, October 12, 2012, in Lexington, Kentucky.

and women's basketball seasons. Now open practices are held earlier in the night and are family affairs.

Similar Midnight Madness events at other colleges have become major recruiting times. Often high school players will verbally commit to a school after attending one of these celebrations.

THE UNIVERSITY OF KENTUCKY CHEERLEADING SQUAD

Though not well documented, the University of Kentucky had cheerleading teams at least as early as 1916. Photos

UNIVERSITY OF KENTUCKY SONGS

Like most universities, the University of Kentucky has traditional songs, the fight song and UK alma mater. But its rich traditions also include this minstrel song composed by Stephen Foster in about 1852:

"My Old Kentucky Home"
The sun shines bright on my old Kentucky home,
'Tis summer, the people are gay;
The corntop's ripe and the meadows in the bloom,
While the birds make music all the day.
The young folks roll on the little cabin floor,
All merry, all happy, and bright;
By-n-by hard times come a-knocking at the door,
Then, my old Kentucky home, good-night!
(CHORUS)
Weep no more, my lady,
Oh! Weep no more, today!
We will sing one song for my old Kentucky home,
For my old Kentucky home far away.

show at least seven men and five women cheerleaders wearing uniforms with SUKY, or State University of Kentucky, as it was known from 1908–1916.

In modern history, no other college cheerleading squad has dominated the Universal Cheerleaders Association (created in 1974) National Championships like the team from Kentucky. The UK squad has won UCA's National College Cheerleading Championship an unprecedented nineteen times, in 1985, 1987, 1988, 1992, 1995, 1996, 1997, 1998, 1999, 2000, 2001, 2002, 2004, 2005, 2006, 2008, 2009, 2010, and 2012—more than any other Division 1A school.

Since 2011, the NCAA has been considering petitions to name cheerleading as an "emerging sport." If approved, cheerleading would become a competitive sport, not just a support for other athletic teams.

WILDCAT MASCOTS

Ross Turner served four years as the UK Wildcat mascot. Turner said one of his favorite times was getting to catch Ashley Judd and spin her around at mid-court.

In the 1970s, mascot costumes were just becoming popular. UK had previously used live wildcats, which often die quickly in captivity. The very first live mascot, "Fuzzy," lived six years and died in 1930.

The Wildcat mascot costume originated during the 1976–1977 academic year at the University of Kentucky. Gary Tanner, 5'9" (175 cm), was the original Wildcat, dancing and entertaining thousands of University of Kentucky fans at Commonwealth Stadium and Rupp Arena during athletics events. The costume was created by Frankfort, Kentucky, native Ann Smith, working for the Act One Theatrical Costume Company in Dayton, Ohio. Each suit lasts two years before it has to be replaced.

A few years later, another Wildcat mascot was added, this time a cat walking on stilts. And today, the original mascot is joined by Scratch, who's a more child-friendly mascot and serves as the host of UK's official kids' club.

1903: First State College (Kentucky) game. Win over Lexington YMCA 11–10. The Wildcats finished the first season with a 1-2 record.

1912: Kentucky defeats Georgetown College 19–18 to complete the season with a perfect 9-0 record and earns its first title as Southern Champions.

1921: Kentucky upsets Tulane, Mercer, Mississippi A&M, and Georgia to win the first Southern Intercollegiate Athletic Association basketball championship.

1933: The University of Kentucky wins the first Southeastern Conference Tournament Championship by defeating Mississippi State 46–27, in Atlanta.

1951: UK wins its third NCAA title, defeating Kansas State, 68–58, in the finals in Minneapolis.

1972: Adolph Rupp coaches his last game at UK, a 73–54 loss to Florida State in the NCAA tournament. The first Midnight Special is held, established by Coach Joe B. Hall.

1985: Eddie Sutton coaches his first game at Kentucky, a 77–58 win over Northwestern LA State.

1989: In the wake of an NCAA investigation, Eddie Sutton resigns as UK basketball coach.

1989: Rick Pitino is named head basketball coach at Kentucky.

1996: After avenging an early-season loss to UMass with a win in the NCAA semifinals two days before, UK squashes a late Syracuse rally to win its sixth national title, 76–67.

1997: UK's director of athletics, C. M. Newton, introduces Orlando "Tubby" Smith as head coach to replace Rick Pitino, who resigned to take over the Boston Celtics.

2009: John Calipari becomes UK's head basketball coach, replacing Billy Gillespie.

2012: The "Eighth Wonders" win the NCAA championship, UK's eighth national championship, with a young team that started three freshmen and two sophomores.

GLOSSARY

ABA The American Basketball Association was a professional basketball league founded in 1967. The ABA ceased to exist with the ABA–NBA merger in 1976.

death penalty When a basketball team breaks NCAA rules, the NCAA penalty may be forfeiting games or an entire season. When the entire season is forfeited, it is a death penalty.

field goal A goal made while the game is in play or when the ball drops through the basket during play.

free throw When a player is fouled, he or she gets a shot at the goal from the free throw line, without any other players in the way.

man-to-man defense A method of defense in which each member of the defensive team is assigned to guard a particular member of the offensive team.

NBA The National Basketball Association is the professional basketball league in the United States.

NCAA The National Collegiate Athletics Association organizes athletic programs at colleges and universities in the United States.

NIT The National Invitational Tournament is a postseason tournament organized by the NCAA.

probation When a basketball team violates NCAA rules, the NCAA may put them on probation. This gives the team a certain period of time to fix problems or mistakes.

recruit To seek new players for a basketball team.

SEC The Southeastern Conference is an American college athletic organization made up of teams mostly in the southeastern part of the United States.

Canadian Collegiate Athletic Association (CCAA)

Association canadienne du sport collégial
2 St. Lawrence Drive
Cornwall, ON K6H 4Z1
Canada
Web site: http://www.ccaa.ca
The CCAA coordinates college sports in Canada, working to develop student athletes.

National Basketball Association

Olympic Tower
645 5th Avenue
New York, NY 10022
(212) 407-8000
Web site: http://www.nba.com
The NBA regulates professional basketball in the United States.

USA Basketball

5465 Mark Dabling Boulevard
Colorado Springs, CO 80918-3842
(719) 590-4800
Web site: http://www.usabasketball.com
The USA Basketball association represents basketball teams in the United States, including the U.S. Olympic teams.

WEB SITES

Due to the changing nature of Internet links, Rosen Publishing has developed an online list of Web sites related to the subject of this book. This site is updated regularly. Please use this link to access the list:

http://www.rosenlinks.com/AMWT/KYBB

FOR FURTHER READING

Adamson, Thomas Kristian. *Basketbal: The Math of the Game.* North Mankato, MN: Capstone Press, 2011.

Christopher, Matt. *Great Moments in Basketball History.* New York, NY: Little, Brown Books for Young Readers, 2010.

Coy, John. *Hoop Genius: How a Desperate Teacher and a Rowdy Gym Class Invented Basketball.* Minneapolis, MN: Carolrhoda, 2013.

Fleder, Rob. *Sports Illustrated: The Basketball Book.* New York, NY: Sports Illustrated, 2007.

Jordan, Deloris. *Dream Big: Michael Jordan and the Pursuit of Olympic Gold.* New York, NY: Simon & Schuster/Paula Wiseman Books, 2012.

Latta, Sara L. *Who Invented Basketball? James Naismith* (I Like Inventors!). Berkeley Heights, NJ: Enslow, 2012.

LeBoutillier, Nate. *The Best of Everything Basketball Book* (Sports Illustrated Kids: The All-Time Best of Sports). North Mankato, MN: Capstone Press, 2011.

LeBoutillier, Nate. *Play Basketball Like a Pro: Key Skills and Tips* (Sports Illustrated Kids: Play Like the Pros). North Mankato, MN: Capstone Press, 2010.

Macy, Sue. *Basketball Belles: How Two Teams and One Scrappy Player Put Women's Hoops on the Map.* New York, NY: Holiday House, 2011.

Slade, Suzanne. Basketball: How It Works (The Science of Sports). North Mankato, MN: Capstone Press, 2010.

BIBLIOGRAPHY

Cave, Ray. "The Old Master Has A New Kind Of Winner." Sports Illustrated, February 19, 1962. SIVault.com. Retrieved December 12, 2012. (http://sportsillustrated.cnn.com/vault/article/magazine/MAG1073546/index.htm)

"Cliff Hagan." Basket-Reference.com, a USA Today Sports Digital property. Retrieval December 12, 2012. (http://www.basketball-reference.com/players/h/hagancl01.html)

"Daniel Paul Issel – bio." NBA History. Retrieved December 12, 2012. (http://www.nba.com/history/players/issel_bio.html)

Deford, Frank. "In Search Of Naismith's Game." SIVault, March 06, 1967. Retrieved December 12, 2012. (http://sportsillustrated.cnn.com/vault/article/magazine/MAG1079595/4/index.htm)

"Frank Ramsey." Big Blue History. Retrieved December 12, 2012. (http://www.bigbluehistory.net/bb/Statistics/Players/Ramsey_Frank.html)

Goldstein, Joe. "Explosion: 1951 scandals threaten college hoops." ESPN Classic. November 13, 2003. Retrieved December 12, 2012. (http://espn.go.com/classic/s/basketball_scandals_explosion.html)

"John Calipari." Official Site of Kentucky Wildcats. University of Kentucky Athletic Department. Retrieved December 12, 2012. (http://www.ukathletics.com/sports/m-baskbl/mtt/calipari_john00.html)

"Kentucky Coaches." Big Blue History. Retrieved December 12. 2012. (http://www.bigbluehistory.net/bb/statistics/coaches.html)

Reed, William F. "One of a Kind Legendary Coach Adolph Rupp—Loved by Some, Loathed by Others—Turned

Kentucky Basketball into a Dynasty." *Sports Illustrated*, Special Issue 0038822X, April 17, 1996, Special Issue

Rick, Russell. Adolph Rupp: Kentucky's Basketball Baron. Urbana, IL: Sagamore Publishing, 1984. ISBN 0-915611-98-8

Story, Mark. "UK's Smith enters Hall having lived the dream." KentuckySports.com. August 13, 2010. Retrieved December 12, 2012. (http://www.kentucky.com/2010/08/13/1390007/mark-story-uks-smith-enters-hall.html).

Tipton, Jerry. Big Blue Madness fans treated to 'The Kentucky Effect'. Kentucky.com website. October 15, 2011. Retrieval December 12, 2012. (http://www.kentucky.com/2011/10/15/1921591/live-now-university-of-kentucky.html).

Tucker, Kyle. "Final Four 2012: For Kentucky basketball fans, nothing but a title will do." Courier-Journal.com. May 30, 2012. Retrieved on December 12, 2012. (http://www.courier-journal.com/article/20120330/SPORTS13/303300119/Final-Four-2012-Kentucky-basketball-fans-nothing-title-will-do?nclick_check=1)

The University of Kentucky Cheerleading Squad. Official Site of the Kentucky Wildcats. Retrieved December 12, 2012. (http://www.ukathletics.com/trads/cheer.html)

"Unparalleled Tradition." University of Kentucky Athletic Department. Kentucky Basketball. Retrieved December 12, 2012. (www.ukathletics.com/doc_lib/mbb_200607mg_084.pdf)

"USA Men's National Team: Games of the XVIIth Olympiad – 1960." The Official Site of USA Basketball. Retrieved December 12, 2012. (http://www.usabasketball.com/mens/national/moly_1960.html)

INDEX

ABOUT THE AUTHOR

Darcy Pattison is an Arkansas Razorback fan and regularly cheers against the Kentucky Wildcats. However, she recognizes the long tradition of winning at the University of Kentucky and applauds any time an SEC team wins big. Pattison writes books for children and teens.

PHOTO CREDITS

Cover, pp. 1, 17 Andy Lyons/Getty Images; back cover (hoop) Mike Flippo/ Shutterstock.com; pp. 4, 39, 40 Joe Robbins/ Getty Images; pp. 5, 10, 12, 14, 22, 28 © AP Images; pp. 6, 11, 20, 27, 36 Chris Graythen/Getty Images; pp. 7, 32 Lee Balterman/ Sports Illustrated/Getty Images; p. 9 Patrick Murphy-Racey/Sports Illustrated/ Getty Images; p. 21 UK Athletics; p. 25 AP Images/Chris Steppig/NCAA Photos, Pool; p. 33 James Drake/Sports Illustrated/Getty Images; p. 35 Hulton Archive/Getty Images; p. 37 Lexington Herald-Leader/ McClatchy-Tribune/ Getty Images; multiple interior page borders and boxed text backgrounds (basketball) Mark Cinotti/Shutterstock.com; back cover and multiple interior pages background (abstract pattern) © iStockphoto.com/ Che McPherson.

Designer: Brian Garvey; Editor: Bethany Bryan; Photo Researcher: Marty Levick